Merry Christmas
Aidan!

This book combines excerpts
from literature that
talk about cooking and their
recipes! Have fun
reading + cooking!

Love,
Steph

Once Upon a Time in the Kitchen

Recipes and Tales from Classic Children's Stories

Carol Odell

Illustrated by Anna Pignataro

Contents

A Message from the Kitchen

When you read a story by a good writer you can sometimes hear and see and smell the story! You know exactly what Pooh sounds like when he is "humming to himself in rather a sticky voice." You can soar away with Peter Pan out of your bed into the night sky. And don't you wish you could have some of the jam tarts from *Alice in Wonderland*?

Now you can eat the food enjoyed by your favorite storybook characters!

Once Upon a Time in the Kitchen gives you the recipes to make the food inspired by famous, well-loved stories.

Here's a tip to remember when cooking: always use your imagination. Add your ideas to the recipes. Never be afraid to make mistakes—sometimes they are just as nice. Be adventurous in trying new things, just like Pinocchio learned to do.

Best of all, enjoy the taste of these lovely stories, and look for the books in libraries and bookstores. They have been around for a long, long time—so they will be waiting …

—Carol Odell

Here is a list of standard kitchen equipment and utensils that you will want to have on hand as you prepare these tasty recipes:

- *assorted large and small mixing bowls*
- *a wooden spoon*
- *a bread knife for spreading and a knife for slicing*
- *scissors*
- *a fork*
- *a tablespoon*
- *a spatula*
- *dry and liquid measuring cups*
- *measuring spoons*
- *a small saucepan*
- *a large baking dish*
- *foil or plastic wrap*
- *waxed paper or paper towel*

If specific equipment or utensils are needed, they are listed in the recipe's **What You Will Need** *section, along with the ingredients.*

Safety First!

Always think carefully when you cook. Adult supervision is advised, particularly when using the oven, hot liquids, or fats.

- Hold sharp knives carefully and watch out for your fingers. Leave plenty of room between the knife and your fingers while holding the vegetable, fruit, or meat you want to chop or slice. If you are walking around the kitchen, hold the knife pointing downward toward the floor—better still, leave it on the table.

- Use wooden spoons for mixing and stirring. A wooden spoon squashes the mixture together more easily and doesn't become hot if you are stirring hot liquids in a pan.

- A flat spatula is what you need for removing fried eggs, pancakes, hamburgers, etc., from the frying pan.

- A round sieve with a handle or a colander can be used for draining liquid from spaghetti, vegetables, etc. If the liquid is hot, lean away as you pour so that you don't get the hot steam in your face.

- A strong plastic or wooden cutting board should be used for cutting, chopping, slicing, rolling out piecrust or shaping biscuits rather than using the kitchen counter. This is so you won't scratch the counter and, because the counter is used for many other things, it's easy to pass germs from one thing to another.

- If you have an electric mixer, blender, and beaters, they will save a lot of time, but be extra careful with your fingers. Never put your fingers inside the bowl! Not only are the blades very sharp—even when they're not whizzing around—but someone else could mistakenly switch the appliance on.

All weights and measurements shown are in standard U.S. units.

Most serving sizes are approximate, depending on whether you are cooking for children or adults, and big or little appetites.

The Voyages of Doctor Dolittle

HUGH LOFTING

Doctor Dolittle was a most unusual doctor because not only did he talk to the animals, but he also understood everything they said to him. He travelled all over the world, and found some very strange-looking animals, and they had some very funny things to say.

"Ah," said the Doctor. "The sausages are done to a turn. Come along—hold your plate near and let me give you some."

Then we sat down at the kitchen table and started a hearty meal.

It was a wonderful kitchen, that. I had many meals there afterwards and I found it a better place to eat in than the grandest dining room in the world. It was so cozy and home-like and warm. It was so handy for the food too. You took it right off the fire, hot, and put it on the table and ate it. And you could watch your toast toasting at the fender and see it didn't burn while you drank your soup. And if you had forgotten to put the salt on the table, you didn't have to get up and go into another room to fetch it; you just reached round and took the big wooden box off the dresser behind you. Then the fireplace—the biggest fireplace you ever saw—was like a room in itself. You could get right inside it even when the logs were burning and sit on the wide seats on either side and roast chestnuts after the meal was over—or listen to the kettle singing, or tell stories, or look at picture-books by the light of the fire. It was a marvellous kitchen. It was like the Doctor, comfortable, sensible, friendly and solid.

"Have another sausage?"

The Doctor turned and said a few words to the dog and duck in some strange talk and signs. They seemed to understand him perfectly.

"Can you talk in squirrel language?" I asked.

"Oh yes. That's quite an easy language," said the Doctor. "You could learn that yourself without a great deal of trouble."

Do-very-little Sausages

Sausages at breakfast are delicious served with eggs and toast. Poke the sausages with a fork to help the fat run out or—to let them cook more quickly—slit them with a knife along their length before you put them under the broiler. If you are barbecuing or camping, cook the sausages on a stick over the campfire. Doctor Dolittle made toast by holding the bread on a fork in front of a fire. If you do this, be very careful not to toast yourself. A long barbecue fork is a good idea, if you have one.

MAKES ENOUGH FOR THE WHOLE FAMILY

WHAT YOU WILL NEED

*a broiler and broiling pan
or a barbecue grill*

INGREDIENTS

*2 sausages per adult,
1 sausage per small child*

1. Turn on the broiler.
2. While it is heating, prepare your sausages for cooking. If they are still connected in one string, cut them apart at each twist so you have single sausages.
3. Arrange sausages on a broiler pan and place the pan under the broiler, or arrange the sausages directly on the barbecue grill. Cook for 10 minutes, turning frequently, or until sausages are golden and cooked through.

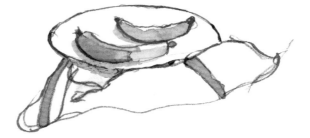

VARIATIONS

Use a knife to split the sausages lengthwise (but don't cut them through completely) and place a long chunk of cheese in each. You can also bind the sausages by wrapping a strip of bacon around each one. The cheese will melt and the bacon will cook nicely while your sausages are being broiled or grilled.

The Jungle Book

RUDYARD KIPLING

The green jungle is home to Mowgli, a boy brought up by a pack of wolves. He knows and loves all animals, understands how they live, how they feel, whether they are hurt or angry. He lies in the sun with them, hides in their dark dens, hunts in the shadows, and shares his food with them all.

Now you must be content to skip ten or eleven whole years, and only guess at all the wonderful life that Mowgli led among the wolves, because if it were written out it would fill ever so many books. He grew up with the cubs, though they, of course, were grown wolves almost before he was a child, and Father Wolf taught him his business, and the meaning of things in the jungle, till every rustle in the grass, every breath of the warm night air, every note of the owls above his head, every scratch of a bat's claws as it roosted for a while in a tree, and every splash of every little fish jumping in a pool, meant just as much to him as the work of his office means to a business man.

When he was not learning he sat out in the sun and slept, and ate and went to sleep again; when he felt dirty or hot he swam in the forest pools; and when he wanted honey (Baloo told him that honey and nuts were just as pleasant to eat as raw meat) he climbed up for it, and that Bagheera showed him how to do. Bagheera would lie out on a branch and call, "Come along, Little Brother," and at first Mowgli would cling like the sloth, but afterward he would fling himself through the branches almost as boldly as the gray ape. He took his place at the Council Rock, too, when the Pack met, and there he discovered that if he stared hard at any wolf, the wolf would be forced to drop his eyes, and so he used to stare for fun. At other times he would pick the long thorns out of the pads of his friends, for wolves suffer terribly from thorns and burs in their coats.

Mowgli Magnificent Muesli

No supermarkets or grocery stores for Mowgli. He had to find his own food, so think of Mowgli as you put your fruit, nuts, and seeds in a bowl and, as you stir them up together, imagine which jungle animals would like to share the mixture with you—then make sure they're not in the kitchen with you!

MAKES 4–5 CUPS MUESLI

WHAT YOU WILL NEED

an airtight container

INGREDIENTS

1 cup rolled oats

1 cup chopped dried fruit (raisins, apples, apricots, etc.)

¼ cup wheat germ

¼ cup lecithin meal

¼ cup bran

¼ cup crushed nuts

¼ cup sesame seeds

¼ cup sunflower seeds

¼ cup skim milk powder

cold milk and honey to serve

Don't worry if you don't have all the ingredients listed for this recipe. Just put in what you do have and it will still make a really good breakfast.

1. Except for the cold milk and honey, mix all the ingredients together in a mixing bowl and stir with a spoon or your clean hands.
2. Store the muesli in an airtight container to share with a pack of hungry brothers, sisters, and parents.

At breakfast time (or any other time) tip some of the muesli into a bowl, pour on some cold milk, and drizzle a little honey over the top. You can also eat it dry and crunchy, without the milk and honey, if you prefer.

The Secret Garden

FRANCES HODGSON BURNETT

Mary lived in India, but when her parents died she was sent to England to live with her uncle and cousin, Colin, in Misselthwaite Manor. By watching a robin fly over a high wall she discovers the entrance to a secret garden, "the sweetest, most mysterious place anyone could imagine." It has been locked since her aunt, Colin's mother, died. Mary meets the country boy, Dickon, "with cheeks as red as poppies," and he becomes her special friend. In the garden Mary, Dickon, and Colin find magic.

Dickon made the stimulating discovery that in the wood in the park, outside the garden where Mary had first found him piping to the wild creatures, there was a deep little hollow where you could build a sort of oven with stones, and roast potatoes and eggs in it. Roasted eggs were a previously unknown luxury and very hot potatoes with salt and fresh butter in them were fit for a wood and king, besides being deliciously satisfying. You could buy both potatoes and eggs and eat as many as you liked.

Every beautiful morning the magic was worked by the mystic circle under the plum tree, which provided a canopy of thickening green leaves after its brief blossom time was over. It became possible for Colin and Mary to do more of their exercises each time they tried, and such appetites were the result that but for the basket Dickon put down behind the bush each morning when he arrived, they would have been lost. But the little oven in the hollow and Mrs. Sowerby's bounties were so satisfying that Mrs. Medlock, the nurse, and Dr. Craven became mystified again. You can trifle with your breakfast and seem to disdain your dinner if you are full to the brim with roasted eggs and potatoes and richly frothed new milk and oatcakes and buns and heather honey and clotted cream.

Secret Garden Two-tone Smoothie

Somehow, milk tastes so much nicer when it's "richly frothed" and nothing is easier to make than a tasty and healthy smoothie for breakfast or anytime.

MAKES 1 LARGE SMOOTHIE OR 2 SMALLER ONES

WHAT YOU WILL NEED

an electric blender or food processor

3 large glasses

a helper for pouring

INGREDIENTS

1 banana and ½ cup berries (or any two fruits of different colors)

4–8 prunes (optional)

1 tablespoon honey

2 tablespoons plain yogurt

2 cups milk (or soy milk)

1. Combine the banana with half of these ingredients (prunes, honey, yogurt, and milk) in an electric blender or food processor. Beat until frothy and pour into a glass.
2. Combine the berries and the other half of the remaining ingredients in the electric blender or food processor and beat until frothy. Pour into a separate glass.
3. Ask someone to help you pour. With each person holding one smoothie, slowly pour the two smoothies into opposite sides of a large glass at the same time to make a two-tone smoothie!

VARIATIONS

Two-fruit smoothies need not be two-tone and they'll still taste just as nice. Combine any two fruits in the blender. Mangoes, berries, and peaches are always great. Instead of all milk, try a combination of milk and fruit nectar or juice.

The Cinnamon Tree in the Moon

TRADITIONAL CHINESE FAIRY TALE

The Moon Festival in China is held on the fifteenth night of the eighth month when the moon is full. Some say there is a mysterious shadow on the moon that night.

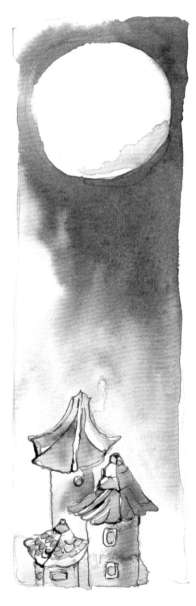

Thousands of years ago, a beautiful full moon shone in the dark night sky. It was so round and so bright many people left their houses and went outside to gaze in wonder. Children, too, scrambled out of their beds, calling out excitedly as they saw shadows on the silver moon. Suddenly, there was a loud swishing noise as something fell to earth, and the children rushed to see what had fallen from the sky.

They came back dragging a large branch of a tree. How could this have happened? There were no trees nearby.

"It will be good to burn on the fire," said one man, "and it will keep my family warm for a night or two."

They carried it back to the house, cut the branch into pieces and put it on the fire. It seemed to burn as brightly as the moon itself but, far stranger, it never stopped burning. It burnt for hours, days, and months, heating the house for the entire winter. And never once did the wood turn to ash.

The family, who were very poor, marvelled at their good fortune, and the story of "the mysterious branch that fell from the sky and never stopped burning" became known throughout the land.

One day, some visiting monks from a far-off monastery came by and said to the family:

"It is a branch of the cinnamon tree that grows on the moon. It has fallen from the sky and brought you great good fortune. If you had made a chest from the cinnamon wood, then you would have found it always full of clothes; if you had made a barrel from the cinnamon wood, then it would have been full of rice; and if you had made a money box from the cinnamon wood, then it would have been full of money for the rest of your life."

Everyone was amazed that such a thing had happened and, that is why to this very day, people gaze at the moon on the fifteenth night of the eighth month, hoping a branch of the cinnamon tree will fall to the ground and bring them good fortune forever.

Cinnamon Moons

Did you know cinnamon was imported from China as far back as 2000 B.C. and was said to grow in swamps protected by flying dragons with sharp claws? Today, cinnamon is used in cakes, biscuits, and puddings and smells wonderful as it heats up and fills the kitchen with its spicy scent.

MAKES 8–10 MOONS, DEPENDING ON THE SIZE OF YOUR BREAD

WHAT YOU WILL NEED

a cookie cutter or lid from a jar

a small frying pan

a large, flat plate or board

INGREDIENTS

4 or 6 slices of bread, depending on size of the moons you are going to cut

1 egg

2 tablespoons milk

2 tablespoons butter or oil

4 tablespoons raw, brown, or white sugar

1 tablespoon cinnamon

1. Cut crusts from bread. Using a round cookie cutter or a lid from a jar, cut round moons from the bread.
2. Crack the egg open and pour into a small bowl. Beat with a fork until the yolk and white are well mixed, then add milk, and pour the mixture onto a large plate. Soak the moons in this for a minute or two.
3. Heat butter or oil in a frying pan and, using a spatula, lift the moons into the pan. When one side is brown, turn over and brown the other side. This happens quite quickly so watch that it doesn't burn.
4. Mix the sugar and cinnamon together in a bowl and spread out on a flat plate or board.
5. Roll the hot moons over and over in the sugar and cinnamon mix. Some will fall off, but enough should stick. Eat while hot.

VARIATION

The bread may be toasted first before cutting out the moons. Then soak, fry, and roll in sugar and cinnamon as before. This makes very crunchy moons. You can always sprinkle extra cinnamon over the moons before serving them, but make sure other people like it first.

The Adventures of Huckleberry Finn

MARK TWAIN

Huckleberry Finn was a boy who was free and easy, and he liked nothing better than making rafts and going fishing with his best friend. They explored the river, swam, laughed, and shared their food together. You can enjoy it too, and without even leaving home.

I never felt easy till the raft was two mile below there and out in the middle of the Mississippi. Then we hung up our signal lantern, and judged that we was free and safe once more. I hadn't had a bit to eat since yesterday; so Jim he got out some corn-dodgers and butter-milk, and pork and cabbage, and greens—there ain't nothing in the world so good, when it's cooked right—and whilst I eat my supper we talked, and had a good time. I was powerful glad to get away from the feuds, and so was Jim to get away from the swamp. We said there warn't no harm like a raft, after all. Other places do seem so cramped up and smothery, but a raft don't. You feel might free and easy and comfortable on a raft.

Huckleberry Corn Rafts

Corn rafts are best eaten piping hot for breakfast, lunch, or dinner. Make extras if you'd also like them cold as a Huckleberry Finn lunch at school (especially if you have a raft of friends).

MAKES 10 CORN RAFTS

WHAT YOU WILL NEED

a frying pan

INGREDIENTS

¾ cup milk

1 teaspoon vinegar

2 eggs, beaten

1 cup self-raising flour

½ teaspoon baking soda

1 (14-ounce) can of corn, drained

2 tablespoons melted butter

oil for frying

1. In a small bowl, stir the milk and vinegar together and set aside for 10 minutes (this makes the milk sour, but don't worry, the end result doesn't taste sour).
2. Add the beaten eggs to the soured milk and stir with a fork to mix.
3. Combine the flour and baking soda in a mixing bowl and slowly add the milk mixture, stirring well to mix.
4. Add the corn and stir with a wooden spoon.
5. Add the melted butter and mix well.
6. Pour a small amount of oil into a medium-hot frying pan and drop spoonfuls of corn mixture into the pan.
7. After 2 or 3 minutes, when bubbles appear on the top, use a spatula or slotted spoon to turn the corn rafts over carefully and cook the other side until golden brown. Be careful they don't burn!
8. Remove the rafts from the pan and place on a hot plate.
9. Cook the remaining corn rafts and eat while hot.

The Town Mouse and the Country Mouse

FROM AESOP'S FABLES

*The Town Mouse loved his rich, comfortable city life, surrounded by bright lights
and the most delicious scraps of food right at his door … but there were dangers.
The Country Mouse loved his quiet, peaceful country life, surrounded by darkness
at night except for the moon and the stars … but he often went hungry.*

It was late in the evening when they crept stealthily into the city, and midnight ere they reached the great house where the Town Mouse took up his quarters. Here were couches of crimson velvet, carvings in ivory, everything in short that denoted wealth and luxury. On the table were the remains of a splendid banquet, to procure which all the choicest shops in the town had been ransacked the day before.

It was now the turn of the courtier to play the host; he places his country friend on purple, runs to and fro to supply all his wants, presses dish upon dish and dainty upon dainty, and, as though he were waiting on a king, tastes every course ere he ventures to place it before his rustic cousin. The Country Mouse, for his part, affects to make himself quite at home, and blesses the good fortune that has wrought such a change in his way of life; when, in the midst of his enjoyment, as he is thinking with contempt of the poor fare he has forsaken, on a sudden the door flies open and a party of revellers, returning from a late entertainment, bursts into the room. The affrighted friends jump from the table in the greatest consternation and hide themselves in the first corner they can reach. No sooner do they venture to creep out again than the barking of dogs drives them back in still greater terror than before. At length, when things seemed quiet, the Country Mouse stole out from his hiding-place, and bidding his friend good-bye, whispered in his ear,

"Oh, my good sir, this fine mode of living may do for those who like it; but give me my barley bread in peace and security before the daintiest feast where Fear and Care are in waiting."

Cheese Pillows

The smell of cheese cooking is nice whether you are a mouse or not. Mice know a good thing when it comes to cheese: try sprinkling grated cheese on vegetables that you don't really like— it will change the taste like magic. Be careful a mouse doesn't eat it before you do!

MAKES 1 MEDIUM-SIZE PILLOW,
TO BE DIVIDED INTO 5–6 NIBBLE-SIZE PORTIONS

WHAT YOU WILL NEED

a small saucepan

INGREDIENTS

1 tablespoon butter or margarine

1 slice of white or brown bread crumbled with your clean hands

1 ¾ ounces (about ¼ cup) grated cheese

1 egg, beaten

salt and pepper

1. In a small saucepan over low heat, slowly melt the butter or margarine.
2. Keep the saucepan on low heat as you stir in the bread crumbs and cheese, and mash together until melted.
3. Add the egg, salt, and pepper, stirring and mixing all the time. The egg will cook faster than the cheese so it looks a bit funny until it's cooked and turns into a soft and sticky little puffy round pillow. Turn it over and over so that it cooks through.
4. Scoop it out onto a plate and eat it with toast or crackers—but share it with about four friends—it's too much for one, unless you are a very hungry mouse. Eat hot or cold.

Treasure Island

ROBERT LOUIS STEVENSON

*"Yo-ho-ho, and a bottle of rum!" Experience the frightening storms at sea, and
"the waves boiling white" with Jim Hawkins who sailed to bare and stony Treasure Island.
Meet Long John Silver, with the parrot sitting on his shoulder, and Ben Gunn, marooned
and alone. And was the treasure ever found?*

Of all the beggar-men that I had seen or fancied, he was the chief for raggedness. He was clothed with tatters of old ship's canvas and old sea cloth; and this extraordinary patchwork was all held together by a system of the most various and incongruous fastenings—brass buttons, bits of stick, and loops of tarry gaskin. About his waist he wore an old brass-buckled leather belt, which was the one thing solid in his whole accoutrement.

"Three years!" I cried. "Were you shipwrecked?"

"Nay, mate," said he. "Marooned."

I had heard the word, and I knew it stood for a horrible kind of punishment common enough among the buccaneers, in which the offender is put ashore with a little powder and shot, and left behind on some desolate and distant island.

"Marooned three years agone," he continued, "and lived on goats since then, and berries, and oysters. Wherever a man is, says I, a man can do for himself. But, mate, my heart is sore for Christian diet. You mightn't happen to have a piece of cheese about you, now? No? Well, many's the long night I've dreamed of cheese—toasted mostly—and woke up again, and here I were."

"If ever I can get aboard again," said I, "you shall have cheese by the stone."

Marooned Cheese Toast

Take your toast and maroon yourself in a really uncomfortable place: a hard chair in the hot sunshine; the bare floor on a cold day; a rock or pile of stones in the garden to experience just a little of what it was like on Treasure Island. Then eat your luscious, hot, soft cheese on crunchy toast …

MAKES 2 SERVINGS

WHAT YOU WILL NEED	**INGREDIENTS**
a toaster	*2 slices bread*
a cheese grater	*2 teaspoons butter or margarine*
a broiler and broiling pan	*4 heaping tablespoons grated cheese*
	½ teaspoon mustard
	1 teaspoon Worcestershire sauce
	1 tablespoon milk or cream
	a little pepper

1. Lightly toast the bread.
2. In a small bowl, mix together the butter or margarine, cheese, mustard, Worcestershire sauce, and milk or cream.
3. Spread over the toast.
4. Place under the broiler for 3 or 4 minutes.
5. Sprinkle with pepper.
6. Serve hot.

The Wind in the Willows

KENNETH GRAHAME

Mole, Rat, Badger, and Toad were four good friends, living by the river and the Wild Woods. "Oh my! Oh my!" Mole was always saying. And Rat, who owned a boat, said, "There is nothing— absolutely nothing—half as much worth doing as simply messing about in boats."

"Look here! If you've really nothing else on hand this morning, supposing we drop down the river together, and have a long day of it?"

The Mole waggled his toes from sheer happiness, spread his chest with a sigh of full contentment, and leaned back blissfully into the soft cushions. "What a day I'm having!" he said. "Let us start at once!"

"Hold hard a minute, then!" said the Rat. He looped the painter through a ring in his landing-stage, climbed up into his hole above, and after a short interval reappeared staggering under a fat, wicker luncheon-basket.

"Shove that under your feet," he observed to the Mole, as he passed it down into the boat. Then he untied the painter and took the sculls again.

"What's inside it?" asked the Mole, wriggling with curiosity.

"There's cold chicken inside it," replied the Rat briefly; "coldtonguecoldhamcoldbeefpickledgherkinssaladfrenchrollscresssandwichespottedmeatgingerbeerlemonadesodawater —"

"O stop, stop," cried the Mole in ecstasies: "This is too much!"

"Do you really think so?" inquired the Rat seriously. "It's only what I always take on these little excursions; and the other animals are always telling me that I'm a mean beast and cut it very fine!"

Mole's Salad in a Breadbasket

withslicedhamchickenboiledeggslettuceonionsgherkinsandcheesehiddeninaloaf

If you are going on a picnic, leave the loaf wrapped until you get there, then unwrap and slice with a bread knife. Watch out for Toad flashing past in his motorcar, tooting his horn.

MAKES 6–8 THICK SLICES

WHAT YOU WILL NEED

clean fingers for scooping

a cheese grater

foil or plastic wrap

INGREDIENTS

1 unsliced small loaf of bread or stick of French bread

1 tablespoon butter or margarine

4–6 lettuce leaves

6 slices ham (less for a small bread loaf)

6 slices cold chicken or other cold meat (or a little less)

3 hard-boiled eggs, shelled and sliced

4 slices onion (optional)

2 pickled gherkins, sliced (optional)

2 tomatoes, sliced

½ cup grated cheese

1. Carefully cut the top crust off the loaf and keep it nearby.
2. Scoop out the soft bread inside, leaving about ⅓ to ½ inch next to the crust.
3. Spread the butter or margarine inside the bread shell.
4. Place a layer of lettuce on the bottom, then a layer of ham, then any other cold meats you have.
5. Add a layer of eggs, then the onion and gherkins.
6. Add the tomatoes, making sure you surround them with lettuce so the bread won't get soggy.
7. Sprinkle the grated cheese over the top. Add enough lettuce to fill to the top.
8. Butter the soft side of the cut-off bread top and place it back on the loaf.
9. Wrap the loaf in foil or plastic wrap and place in the refrigerator with a weight (such as a plate) on top for at least two hours (or even overnight). Slice into thick, sandwich-sized chunks when you are ready to eat.

Winnie-the-Pooh

A. A. MILNE

*Pooh Bear was a very special bear, not only for Christopher Robin who owned him,
but also for Tigger and Piglet and all his friends. He liked to sit and hum songs,
and think about honey. Pooh was a sensible bear, a cheerful bear, and a friendly bear.
No wonder he was an Important Bear who had all sorts of adventures.*

Pooh always liked a little something at eleven o'clock in the morning, and he was very glad to see Rabbit getting out the plates and mugs; and when Rabbit said, "Honey or condensed milk with your bread?" he was so excited that he said, "Both," and then, so as not to seem greedy, he added, "But don't bother about the bread, please." And for a long time after that he said nothing ... until at last, humming to himself in a rather sticky voice, he got up, shook Rabbit lovingly by the paw, and said that he must be going on ....

"Well, good-bye, if you're sure you won't have any more."

"Is there any more?" asked Pooh quickly.

Rabbit took the covers off the dishes, and said, "No, there wasn't."

"I thought not," said Pooh, nodding to himself. "Well, good-bye. I must be going on."

So he started to climb out of the hole ....

"Oh, help!" said Pooh. "I'd better go back."

"Oh bother!" said Pooh. "I shall have to go on."

"I can't do either!" said Pooh. "Oh help and bother!"

Now, by this time Rabbit wanted to go for a walk too, and finding the front door full, he went out by the back door, and came round to Pooh, and looked at him ...

"The fact is," said Rabbit, "you're stuck."

"It all comes," said Pooh crossly, "of not having front doors big enough."

"It all comes," said Rabbit sternly, "of eating too much, I thought at the time," said Rabbit, "only I didn't like to say anything," said Rabbit, "that one of us was eating too much," said Rabbit, "and I knew it wasn't me," he said.

Bear Honey and Nut Spread

"Isn't it funny how a bear likes honey? Buzz! Buzz! Buzz! I wonder why he does?" sang Pooh. Perhaps you have your own cooking song? This spread will make you want to hummmm like Pooh, bounce like Tigger, and sh-shake your ears with excitement, like Piglet.

MAKES A SMALL JARFUL

WHAT YOU WILL NEED

a small jar with a lid

INGREDIENTS

½ cup crushed nuts

4 tablespoons honey

1. Place nuts in a bowl.
2. Add honey and blend until you have a thick paste. It will not be completely smooth as some of the nut pieces will remain firm.
3. Spoon into a small jar and spread on bread or toast.

The Life and Adventures of Robin Hood

JOHN B. MARSH

Robin Hood, who "robbed the rich to give to the poor," enjoyed living in the Greenwood of Sherwood Forest with his Merry Men. They had exciting escapes and dangerous captures, swordfights, hunting with bows and arrows, singing, laughing, and feasting. The sheriff and his men didn't like Robin Hood, and Maid Marian thought it was wrong to take money without asking—however rich the people.

When all had entered, Robin pointing to the king, exclaimed, "Let every man who loves his country and his king say with me, 'God save King Richard!' "

The men seemed to be taken completely aback. They took off their caps, and, waving them in the air, shouted with all their might, "God save King Richard!" Then cheer after cheer rent the air.

The king's countenance changed at the reception he received, and he gave Robin and Little John each a friendly buffet on the shoulder.

When the feast was ready, Robin sent for Marian and Ellen, and presented them to the king, who, as he looked upon their faces, exclaimed, "By my head they are comely dames!"

They sat down on the grass to the feast, and Robin with Little John waited on the king. They had roast venison, river fowl, and flesh of several sorts; besides good bread, old wine, and strong ale.

The king ate heartily, and was very merry over the feast. He told them strange stories of his adventures in the Holy Land, and of his sufferings in captivity.

When the feast was ended, the king filled a horn with wine, and calling upon all present to do likewise, proposed "Long life to Robin Hood and his merry men!"

Sherwood Forest Chicken

MAKES ABOUT 4 SERVINGS

WHAT YOU WILL NEED

a lemon squeezer

tongs

a barbecue grill or broiler and broiler pan

INGREDIENTS

4 chicken thighs (easier to cook than breasts) or 4 drumsticks, or two of each

juice of half a lemon

1 tablespoon olive oil or butter

1. Start the barbecue grill or the broiler.
2. Rub the chicken pieces all over with lemon juice. The drumsticks will take a little longer to cook so put them on first if you are cooking both thighs and drumsticks. Put them on the barbecue grill or under a hot broiler.
3. Brush or drizzle about a third of the olive oil over the chicken, and cook for 5 minutes. Be careful of flames around oil on the barbecue grill.
4. Turn them over, pour half the remaining oil over them, and cook for another 5 minutes.
5. Turn them over again, pour the rest of the oil over them, and cook for 5 minutes. Pierce the meat with a sharp knife or skewer and if the juice is clear the chicken should be cooked and tender. If the juice is pink, cook the chicken a little longer, then test it again.

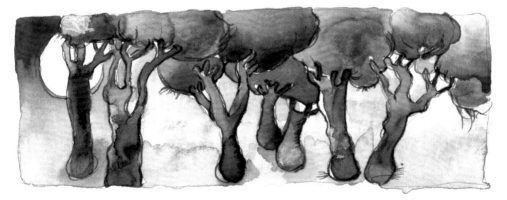

VARIATION
Instead of using olive oil, marinate (soak) the chicken pieces in ¼ cup soy sauce, 1 tablespoon sweet chili sauce, and 1 tablespoon honey. Mix together and spread over the chicken pieces. Leave for 10 minutes or longer.

Little Women

LOUISA MAY ALCOTT

In the old days "nice" girls were not allowed to behave like boys. Jo didn't take any notice of that, because she loved playing boyish games, and often got her sisters in trouble. The family usually forgave her because she was always laughing and enthusiastic and they all loved one another very much.

Language cannot describe the anxieties, experiences, and exertions which Jo underwent that morning; and the dinner she served up became a standing joke. Fearing to ask any more advice, she did her best alone, and discovered that something more than energy and goodwill is necessary to make a cook. She boiled the asparagus for an hour, and was grieved to find the heads cooked off and the stalks harder than ever. The bread burnt black; and the salad dressing so aggravated her, that she let everything else go till she had convinced herself that she could not make it fit to eat. The lobster was a scarlet mystery to her, but she hammered and poked, till it was unshelled, and its meagre proportions concealed in a grove of lettuce leaves. The potatoes had to be hurried, not to keep the asparagus waiting, and were not done at last. The blancmange was lumpy, and the strawberries not as ripe as they looked, having been skillfully "deaconed."

"Well, they can eat beef, and bread and butter, if they are hungry; only it's mortifying to have to spend your whole morning for nothing," thought Jo, as she rang the bell half an hour later than usual, and stood, hot, tired, and dispirited, surveying the feast spread for Laurie, accustomed to all sorts of elegance, and Miss Crocker, whose curious eyes would mark all failures, and whose tattling tongue would report them far and wide.

Poor Jo would gladly have gone under the table, as one thing after another was tasted and left; while Amy giggled, Meg looked distressed, Miss Crocker pursed up her lips, and Laurie talked and laughed with all his might, to give a cheerful tone to the festive scene.

Jo's Perfect Potato Casserole

Jo enjoyed cooking, but sometimes made terrible mistakes. However, as Jo always made the best of everything, she just started cooking all over again. And, there were times when she said that the mistake tasted just as good, but her family wasn't sure whether to agree or not.

MAKES ENOUGH FOR THE WHOLE FAMILY

WHAT YOU WILL NEED

a potato peeler

INGREDIENTS

1 potato per person

nutmeg

salt and pepper

milk, enough to cover potatoes

1. Peel the potatoes and slice thinly. (Be careful of your fingers!)
2. Put the slices into a big, flat baking dish and sprinkle with nutmeg, salt, and pepper, and just cover with milk.
3. Place in the oven and bake at 400°F until brown and bubbly.

The Owl and the Pussy-cat

EDWARD LEAR

*Edward Lear is best known for laughter and nonsense verses: the "Moppsikon Floppsikin Bear";
the "Worrying Whizzing Wasp"; the "Yongby-Bonghy-Bo"; and the "Umrageous Umbrella-man."
And whoever heard of a "Kicking Kangaroo in a pale pink muslin dress"? Or the "Melodious
Meritorious Mouse who played the piano"? Best of all is "The Owl and the Pussy-cat."*

The Owl and the Pussy-cat went to sea
   In a beautiful pea-green boat,
   They took some honey, and plenty of money,
Wrapped up in a five-pound note.
The Owl looked up at the stars above,
And sang to a small guitar,
"O lovely Pussy! O Pussy, my love,
What a beautiful Pussy you are,
     You are,
     You are!
What a beautiful Pussy you are!"
…They dined on mince, and slices of quince,
Which they ate with a runcible spoon;
And hand in hand, on the edge of the sand,
They danced by the light of the moon,
     The moon,
     The moon,
They danced by the light of the moon.

Owls and Pussy-cats in Pea-green Boats

No wonder the Owl and the Pussy-cat took mince in their pea-green boat. Mince, or ground beef, can be made into so many different meals. Best of all, it is eaten "with a runcible spoon" (a fork-like spoon with a cutting edge—invented by Edward Lear).

MAKES 8 LITTLE BOATS (ABOUT 4 SERVINGS)

WHAT YOU WILL NEED

a sharp knife for chopping

a frying pan

a large saucepan

INGREDIENTS

2 tablespoons olive oil

1 red or brown onion

1 stick celery

1 carrot

½ pound ground beef

1 tablespoon flour

½ cup water

1 tablespoon tomato paste (or better still, some sun-dried tomatoes)

salt and pepper

8 small lettuce leaves—such as baby romaine lettuce leaves—and make sure they are clean and crunchy cold

1. Chop the onion, celery, and carrot into small pieces.
2. Put the olive oil into a frying pan over high heat and brown the vegetables.
3. Stir to keep them from burning, then put aside in a saucepan.
4. Cook the ground beef in small amounts so the juice doesn't run out of the meat, and it will turn a tasty brown.
5. Add the meat to the vegetables in the saucepan and stir them together.
6. Sprinkle in flour and mix thoroughly. Add water and stir until it thickens.
7. Add the tomato paste and taste to see how much salt and pepper you need to add.
8. Keep it warm on the lowest heat and spoon the mixture into the lettuce boats. Serve immediately.

Peter Piper

JOHN HARRIS

Tongues can do many things: taste toast, tickle your teeth, lick your lips, feel fudge, sing a song, and speak a sentence. See if your tongue can get around this famous "tongue twister."

Peter Piper pick'd a Peck of Pepper:
Did Peter Piper pick a Peck of Pepper?
If Peter Piper pick'd a Peck of Pepper,
Where's the Peck of Pepper Peter Piper pick'd?

Neddy Noodle nipp'd his Neighbour's Nutmegs:
Did Neddy Noodle nip his Neighbour's Nutmegs?
If Neddy Noodle nipp'd his Neighbour's Nutmegs,
Where are the Neighbour's Nutmegs
     Neddy Noodle nipp'd?

Billy Button bought a butter'd Biscuit:
Did Billy Button buy a butter'd Biscuit?
If Billy Button bought a butter'd Biscuit,
Where's the butter'd Biscuit
     Billy Button bought?

Neddy Noodle's Noodles

Did you know pepper grows as a berry on a vine, is picked when almost ripe, then dried in the sun or over hot coals? Nutmegs are the size and color of apricots. They are harvested with long hooked poles, the husks removed, then the mace (the reddish material covering the nut). When the dried nut is cracked open, there—at last—is the nutmeg.

MAKES ABOUT 4 SERVINGS

WHAT YOU WILL NEED

2 large saucepans

INGREDIENTS

2 tablespoons olive oil

2 large onions, peeled and chopped

1 carrot, sliced

2 sticks celery, sliced (including leaves)

1 clove garlic, chopped

1 pound ground beef

1 (14-ounce) can peeled tomatoes

½ teaspoon dried oregano or fresh oregano leaves

¼ teaspoon dried thyme or two fresh sprigs of thyme

½ teaspoon salt

a few shakes of pepper

noodles or spaghetti, enough for four people

1. Heat the oil in a large saucepan over low heat. Fry onions, carrot, celery, and garlic slowly until onions are soft and pale. Move vegetables to a plate and set aside.
2. Turn up the heat and add ground beef. Stir until it browns.
3. Add tomatoes. Stir, turn down the heat, add oregano, thyme, salt, and pepper. Add vegetables and mix it all together.
4. With a clean spoon, taste to see if the meat mixture needs a little more salt. (Be careful not to burn your mouth!) If the mixture is too thick, add a few spoonfuls of water. Leave on low heat for about 20 minutes, but make sure it doesn't burn on the bottom. Turn off the heat and leave covered in the pan until ready to pour over the noodles.
5. Cook the noodles or spaghetti according to the instructions on the packet.

Robinson Crusoe

DANIEL DEFOE

*A shipwreck in a wild storm is very frightening, but Robinson Crusoe kept his cool and managed
to make a raft from the wreckage. He also rescued some food so that when he was washed onto
a desert island he was able to survive. He was all alone trying to keep alive until one day—
on a Friday—he found someone very special, and he called him his Man Friday.*

My raft was now strong enough to bear any reasonable weight; my next care was what
to load it with, and how to preserve what I laid upon it from the surf of the sea; but I
was not long considering this; I first laid all the planks or boards upon it that I could
get, and having considered well what I most wanted, I first got three of the seamen's chests, which
I had broken open and emptied, and lowered them down upon my raft; the first of these I filled
with provisions, viz. bread, rice, three Dutch cheeses, five pieces of dried goat's flesh, which we
lived much upon, and a little remainder of European corn which had been laid by for some fowls
which we brought to sea with us, but the fowls were killed; there had been some barley and wheat
together, but, to my great disappointment, I found afterwards that the rats had eaten or spoiled
it all; as for liquors, I found several cases of bottles belonging to our skipper, in which were some
cordial waters, and in all above five or six gallons of rack; these I stowed by themselves.

Robinson Crusoe Island Fried Rice

Rice would have helped Robinson Crusoe keep strong and healthy on his desert island. People in many countries eat rice every day—sometimes for two or three meals a day. You could ask a friend to be your Man Friday or Girl Friday and share the cooking with you.

MAKES 4 SERVINGS

WHAT YOU WILL NEED

a saucepan with lid

a frying pan

a cheese grater

INGREDIENTS

2 cups water

1 cube beef or chicken stock (optional)

1 cup rice

1 tablespoon vegetable oil

4 slices bacon, chopped and rind removed

2 onions, peeled and chopped

1 green pepper, chopped

1 tomato, cut into small wedges

¼ teaspoon pepper

½ cup grated cheese (optional)

1. Bring two cups of water to a boil in a saucepan, then add the stock cube and pour in the rice.
2. Put a lid on the saucepan and turn the heat to low. Simmer for 30 minutes, or until all the water has been absorbed into the rice. (This recipe is even nicer if you cook the rice the day before.)
3. While the rice is cooking, heat the oil in a frying pan and when the oil is hot, add the bacon pieces and onions and fry until golden brown.
4. Add the green pepper and continue frying for 2 minutes.
5. Put in the tomato wedges and mix it all together.
6. Take the frying pan off the heat until the rice is ready. When the rice is cooked, heat the frying pan again until it is hot, then pour the rice mix in. Add pepper. Turn the mixture over and over to heat it through, then turn off the heat.
7. Spoon it onto plates and sprinkle with grated cheese.

May be eaten as a meal in itself, as a side dish, or cold with salad.

The Story of Aladdin

REV. G. FYLER TOWNSEND

Aladdin was a boy who owned a special lamp; he had only to rub it and a genie appeared ready to grant his every wish. Aladdin had many magical adventures travelling to faraway places full of color and the scent of spice.

Give me the lamp I brought home with me yesterday; I will go and sell it, and the money I shall get for it will serve both for breakfast and dinner, and perhaps supper too."

Aladdin's mother took the lamp, and said to her son, "Here it is, but it is very dirty; if it was a little cleaner I believe it would bring something more." She took some fine sand and water to clean it; but had no sooner begun to rub it, than in an instant a hideous genie of gigantic size appeared before her, and said to her in a voice of thunder, "What wouldst thou have? I am ready to obey thee as thy slave, and the slave of all those who have that lamp in their hands; I and the other slaves of the lamp."

Aladdin's mother, terrified at the sight of the genie, fainted; when Aladdin, who had seen such a phantom in the cavern, snatched the lamp out of his mother's hand, and said to the genie boldly, "I am hungry, bring me something to eat." The genie disappeared immediately, and in an instant returned with a large silver tray, holding twelve covered dishes of the same metal, which contained the most delicious viands; six large white bread cakes on two plates, two flagons of wine, and two silver cups. All these he placed upon a carpet, and disappeared; this was done before Aladdin's mother recovered from her swoon.

The Genie's Wish Chicken

MAKES ABOUT 4 SERVINGS

WHAT YOU WILL NEED

a baking dish

a small saucepan

INGREDIENTS

2 pounds chicken drumsticks
(or other chicken pieces)

2 tablespoons olive oil

½ cup honey

⅓ cup soy sauce

1 teaspoon ground ginger

1. Preheat the oven to 350°F.
2. Put the chicken and oil in a baking dish.
3. In a small saucepan gently heat the honey, soy sauce, and ginger. (Be careful: if the heat is too high, the sauce will stick to the saucepan.)
4. When the sauce is warm, give it a stir, then pour over the chicken pieces.
5. Bake for an hour.

Also tastes good served with rice.

VARIATION

Use 2 tablespoons peanut butter and ½ cup honey instead of the soy sauce and ginger. Just put the oil in the baking dish, rub or spread the chicken pieces with peanut butter, and drizzle the honey over the top before baking.

Peter Pan

J. M. BARRIE

Peter Pan lives in Neverland, and wants to stay a boy forever. One day he finds the Darling family but loses his shadow. He teaches all the children how to fly, and they follow him out of their bedroom window, high up above the houses, and into a magical world. Here they meet Tinkerbell, the Lost Boys, and the terrifying Captain Hook.

I suppose it was all especially entrancing to Wendy, because those rampageous boys of hers gave her so much to do. Really there were whole weeks when, except perhaps with a stocking in the evening, she was never above ground. The cooking, I can tell you, kept her nose to the pot. Their chief food was roasted breadfruit, yams, coconuts, baked pig, mammee-apples, tappa rolls, and bananas, washed down with calabashes of poe-poe; but you never exactly knew whether there would be a real meal or just a make-believe, it all depended upon Peter's whim. He could eat, really eat, if it was part of a game, but he could not stodge just to feel stodgy, which is what most children like better than anything else; the next best thing being to talk about it. Make-believe was so real to him that during a meal of it you could see him getting rounder. Of course it was trying, but you simply had to follow his head, and if you could prove to him that you were getting loose for your tree he let you stodge.

Neverland Baked Bananas

With Peter Pan you never really knew whether you would get something real or make-believe. So why not use your imagination and make scrumptious food for yourself. Just remember, never, never stodge just to feel stodgy!

MAKES 4 SERVINGS

WHAT YOU WILL NEED

a baking dish

a pastry brush

INGREDIENTS

4 bananas

2 tablespoons vegetable oil or melted butter

2 tablespoons honey or dark brown sugar

cream or ice cream, to serve

1. Preheat the oven to 350°F.
2. Brush a little of the oil in the bottom of a baking dish.
3. Peel the bananas and place them in the dish.
4. Pour in the rest of the oil, then drizzle the honey over the bananas (or sprinkle with sugar).
5. Bake in the oven for about 15 minutes or until the bananas are quite soft.
6. Serve with cream or ice cream.

VARIATION

Bananas may also be baked in their skins. Slit them open with a knife when they are cooked and eat the hot fruit with a spoon. Be careful; the fruit can be very hot.

Pinocchio

CARLO COLLODI · TRANSLATED BY JOSEPH WALKER

Pinocchio is a puppet carved out of wood by Gepetto who longed for a boy of his own.
Pinocchio's friends Cat, Talking Cricket, and others take him on amazing adventures.
Pinocchio finds out that telling lies may make your nose grow longer.

His story was much mixed, but Gepetto caught the main point in it, which was the fact that the marionette was hungry. So he took three pears out of his pocket, saying, "Here are some pears which were to have been my own breakfast, but I will gladly give them to you. Eat them and may they do you good."

"If you want me to eat them, please peel them for me."

"Peel them?" replied Gepetto in surprise. "I would never have thought, my boy, that you would be so hard to please. One has to get used to all sorts of things in this world."

"You may be right," replied Pinocchio; "but I don't intend to eat any fruit that isn't peeled. I don't like the skins."

At this the good Gepetto took out a small knife and patiently peeled the three pears, laying all the peeling on a corner of the table.

When Pinocchio had eaten the first pear, he was on the point of throwing away the core, but Gepetto stopped him.

"Don't throw that away," he said; "everything is of some use."

"But I don't propose to eat cores."

"Very well," replied his father calmly.

But the cores, instead of being thrown away, were placed on the corner of the table with the parings.

Having eaten, or rather gobbled, the three pears, Pinocchio yawned and said with a whine,

"Oh dear, I am still hungry!"

"I haven't anything else, my boy."

"Really, truly nothing?"

"Nothing except these peeling and cores."

"All right then," said Pinocchio; "I guess I'd better eat some peeling."

He began to eat—at first with a wry face—but one after another the skins went down. Then he tackled the cores, and when he had finished the lot he said, patting his stomach contentedly, "Ah, I feel better!"

"You see, then," observed Gepetto, "that I was right when I told you everything was of some use in this world."

Pinocchio Pears

Pinocchio refused to eat fruit that wasn't peeled—one of the best parts of pears and apples—but for this recipe he is right, and the pears need to be peeled. If you're as hungry as Pinocchio you can eat the peelings. Otherwise, add them to your garden compost heap to feed the hungry garden worms.

MAKES 4 SERVINGS

WHAT YOU WILL NEED

a baking dish

INGREDIENTS

4 large pears

½ cup white or green grapes or chopped raisins

2 tablespoons marmalade

¼ cup water

1. Preheat the oven to 350°F.
2. Peel the pears, leaving them whole.
3. With a small knife, cut around the stems and dig into the pears carefully to remove the cores.
4. Stuff the grapes and marmalade into the holes where the cores were and put the pears into a baking dish. If there is any of the stuffing left over, put it into the bottom of the dish.
5. Pour the water into the dish.
6. Bake in the oven for 1 hour.

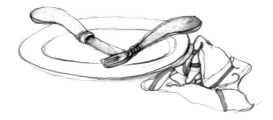

The Water Babies

CHARLES KINGSLEY

Tom was a little chimney sweep who, with his long brush, cleaned the inside of dark, narrow, sooty chimneys. "He cried half the time, and laughed the other half." He longed for water in which to get clean and, one day, found himself in the deep sea where there are some very strange things. He learns many lessons in how to behave kindly to the sea creatures, and meets Mrs. Bedonebyasyoudid and her sister Madame Doasyouwouldbedoneby.

And Tom longed to go to the cabinet, and yet he was afraid; and then he longed again, and was less afraid; and at last, by continual thinking about it, he longed so violently, that he was not afraid at all. And one night, when all the other children were asleep, and he could not sleep for thinking of lollipops, he crept away among the rocks, and got to the cabinet, and behold! It was open.

But, when he saw all the nice things inside, instead of being delighted, he was quite frightened, and wished he had never come there. And then he would only touch them, and he did; and then he would only taste one, and he did; and then he would only eat one, and he did; and then he would only eat two, and then three, and so on; and then he was terrified lest she should come and catch him, and began gobbling them down so fast that he did not taste them, or have any pleasure in them; and then he felt sick, and would only have one more; and then only one more again; and so on till he had eaten them all up.

And all the while, close behind him, stood Mrs. Bedonebyasyoudid.

Watermelon Boat

Pink watermelon balls frozen in the freezer make perfect iced lollipops. Did you know watermelon is 92% water, and if you squeezed all the water out of the fruit you'd get around ½ cup of pink water? The Water Babies would have felt quite at home in a watermelon boat.

MAKES ABOUT 6 SERVINGS (OR HALVE THE INGREDIENTS FOR 3 SERVINGS)

WHAT YOU WILL NEED

a melon baller or teaspoon

INGREDIENTS

½ a watermelon (it is very hard to cut, so if it is not pre-cut to size, ask someone to cut it lengthwise for you)

1 papaya or cantaloupe

1 cup pitted cherries (fresh or canned)

1 cup lychees (canned)

1 cup strawberries

handful of mint leaves

½ cup thick yogurt (use more if you wish)

a sprinkle of raw sugar (optional)

1. With a melon baller (or a teaspoon), take out the red flesh of the watermelon and put it in a large bowl. Don't throw away the shell that's left!
2. Do the same with the papaya or cantaloupe (but throw away their shells).
3. Drain the cherries and lychees and add them to the bowl (you can save the juice to make ice blocks).
4. Pick stems and leaves from the strawberries, then add the berries to the bowl.
5. Stir fruit together and then pile into the watermelon basket.
6. Decorate with mint leaves and blobs of yogurt. Sprinkle with a little raw sugar for glitter if you wish.

Alice's Adventures in Wonderland

LEWIS CARROLL

When Alice fell down a rabbit hole she found a very curious world.
She could grow larger and smaller, the Queen kept saying "Off with her head,"
and many in Court were playing cards that had come alive.

The King and Queen of Hearts were seated on their throne when they arrived, with a great crowd assembled about them—all sorts of little birds and beasts, as well as the whole pack of cards: the Knave was standing before them, in chains, with a soldier on each side to guard him; and near the King was the White Rabbit, with a trumpet in one hand, and a scroll of parchment in the other. In the very middle of the court was a table, with a large dish of tarts upon it: they looked so good that it made Alice quite hungry to look at them—"I wish they'd get the trial done," she thought, "and hand round the refreshments!" But there seemed to be no chance of this, so she began looking about her, to pass away the time.

Alice had never been in a court of justice before, but she had read about them in books, and she was quite pleased to find that she knew the name of nearly everything there. "That's the judge," she said to herself, "because of his great wig."

The judge, by the way, was the King; and as he wore his crown over the wig … he did not look at all comfortable, and it was certainly not becoming.

"And that's the jury-box," thought Alice, "and those twelve creatures," (she was obliged to say "creatures," you see, because some of them were animals, and some were birds) "I suppose they are the jurors." She said this last word two or three times over to herself, being rather proud of it: for she thought, and rightly too, that very few little girls of her age knew the meaning of it at all.

The Queen of Hearts' Jam Tarts

Jam tarts make people feel happy, so perhaps they should be in all courts, police stations, offices, and serious places. Prepare a big plateful to make someone deliciously happy, wherever they are.

MAKES ABOUT 12 TARTS

WHAT YOU WILL NEED

a 12-cup muffin tin

INGREDIENTS

2 sheets frozen piecrust, thawed, or use ready-made pastry cases

a walnut-size knob of butter or margarine

raspberry jam or other jam

1. Preheat the oven to 430°F.
2. Put a little butter or margarine on waxed paper or a paper towel, and rub it over the insides of the muffin cups.
3. To make tart cases: cut circles out of the pie crust sheets to fit the muffin cups, then gently press one into each muffin cup so that the pastry sits on the base of the cup and up the sides to the top edge. Trim off any excess pastry by pressing your finger along the top edge. (Or use the ready-made pastry cases.)
4. Put a teaspoonful of jam in the middle of each tart case.
5. Bake in the oven for 10–15 minutes.

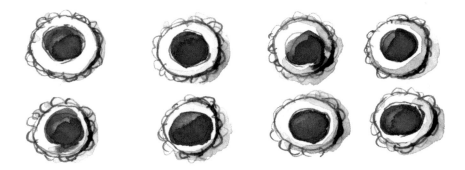

The Fir Tree

HANS CHRISTIAN ANDERSEN

This is a story by one of the greatest happy/sad fairy tale writers in the world.
This one is about a fir tree that was sad to be cut down, but birds told him of beautifully
decorated Christmas trees they had seen through the windows of houses.

A short time before Christmas the fir tree was the first to fall as the axe cut through the stem and divided the pith; the tree fell with a groan to the earth, conscious of pain and faintness, and forgetting all its anticipation of happiness in sorrow at leaving its home in the forest. It knew that it should never see again its near companions the trees, nor the little bushes and many-coloured flowers that had grown by its side; perhaps not even the birds.

Neither was the journey very pleasant.

But then came two servants in grand livery and carried the fir tree into a large and beautiful room. The fir tree was placed in a large tub of sand, with green baize hung all around it so that no one could see it was in a tub.

How the fir tree trembled!

"What is going to happen to me now?"

Then the servants and young ladies decked it out by hanging little bags of coloured paper from its branches, each bag filled with sweetmeats. From other branches they hung gilded apples and walnuts, as if they had grown there. And above and all around were red, blue and white candles fastened to the branches. Dolls that looked like real babies—the fir tree had never seen such things before—hung among the green foliage, and at the very top they fastened a glittering star made of tinsel. Oh, it was very beautiful.

"This evening," said all, "this evening the star will shine!"

Shortbread Stars

Wrap your shortbread stars in gold or silver foil to keep them fresh as well as making them look shiny bright. They'll look pretty for parties or make glorious gifts—all the more special because you made them.

MAKES ABOUT 30 SMALL STARS OR 4 LARGE STARS

WHAT YOU WILL NEED

a small saucepan

a sieve or flour sifter

a rolling pin

a pastry board or cutting board

a cookie cutter in a star shape

a baking sheet

INGREDIENTS

1 ¾ sticks butter, softened in a saucepan over very low heat

⅓ cup superfine sugar

½ cup rice flour

1 ⅓ cup plain flour

½ cup ground almonds or hazelnuts

pinch of salt

1. Preheat the oven to 325°F.
2. Using a wooden spoon, mix the butter and sugar in a large bowl and beat until creamy.
3. Sift together the flours, combine with the butter mixture, and add the nuts and salt. This might be crumbly but press it together in your hands and put it on a board.
4. Roll it out flat to about ⅓ inch thick and either cut out stars with a star cutter or cut with a knife into a large star. Any scraps can be pressed together and rolled out again. Try to get all the stars the same thickness to avoid any thin stars overcooking before the thicker ones are cooked through.
5. Grease the baking sheet with a little softened butter and bake the stars in the oven for about 30 minutes or until light golden brown.
6. Leave on the tray for a few minutes before placing on a wire rack to cool completely.

If you don't want to wrap your shortbread stars in foil, sprinkle them with stardust (icing sugar).

Beauty and The Beast

CHARLES PERRAULT

Once there was a loving father with three daughters, one of whom was called Beauty.
On his travels, the father found a great palace and, as he picked a rose to take home,
an ugly beast appeared. Later, when Beauty heard her father's story, she was
sorry for the lonely, unhappy beast and went to visit him.

From behind a nearby bush there came a piteous sigh. Then a terrible voice rang out, wild and snarling. At first she was filled with horror and not a little afraid but she mastered her fear and as she listened to his words, so wise and kind, her heart grew lighter.

From that time forth they conversed throughout the day—the beauty and the beast. His snarling voice made her afraid no longer and they would hold long conversations from dawn to dusk.

Time passed. But there came a day when the merchant's youngest daughter longed to see the beast with her own eyes. Again she began to beg and beseech him. For a long time he did not consent, afraid that she would hate him once she set eyes on his repulsive form. Yet he couldn't endure her tears and at last yielded to her pleas.

"I cannot go against your wishes, since I love you more than I care for myself," said the beast. "I will grant your wish, but I know it may destroy us both. Come to the gardens in the shadows of the dusk and say—show yourself to me, dear friend."

Unalarmed and unafraid, she went directly to the garden at the appointed hour and, as the sun was sinking low, she called, "Show yourself to me, dear friend."

At a distance, the beast showed himself to her. But fleetingly. He quickly moved across the path and disappeared into the bushes. At once she let out a cry of horror and swooned upon the ground, so horrible indeed was that awful creature.

When the maid regained her senses, she heard sobbing as if a heart would break. She felt ashamed and sorry. Mastering her timid heart, she spoke up firmly. "Do not weep, my friend, I fear your form no longer. Your ugly shape is not your doing: true beauty lies within, not in what is without."

From that day forth, they walked and talked together in trust and wisdom; and the merchant's daughter slowly lost her fear. All day they were together. At breakfast and dinner they ate their fill of sweetmeats and refreshed themselves with meads and sherbets.

Beautiful Fruit Sweets

MAKES ABOUT 30 SLICES AND 15–20 FRUIT BALLS

WHAT YOU WILL NEED

a medium saucepan

a blender or food processor

a pastry board or cutting board

INGREDIENTS

1 cup prunes, drained (canned or dried)

1 cup dried figs

1 cup seedless raisins or white or green grapes

½ cup chopped nuts (walnuts, peanuts, or mixed nuts)

½ cup coconut or finely chopped nuts

1. If you are using dried prunes, first cover them with water and simmer slowly in a saucepan over low heat for 10 minutes. Drain, cool, and remove any stones.
2. Rinse figs and raisins or grapes and dry thoroughly.
3. Using a blender or food processor, grind the nuts and fruit until finely chopped.
4. Remove from the blender and place in a bowl. Blend the mixture together with your clean fingers until it is smooth.
5. Divide half the mixture and, using your hands, shape it and roll it into a smooth log.
6. Sprinkle the coconut or finely chopped nuts onto a pastry board or cutting board. Roll the log over and over on the board, then chill it in the fridge before cutting it into slices.
7. Shape the other half of the mixture into small balls, rolling them in the palms of your hands until round and smooth. Roll in coconut or nuts, and chill until they are firm.

These fruit sweets can be kept for several weeks. Wrap them in foil or colored plastic wrap, or roll them in sprinkles.

For my youngest grandsons, Martin and Lachlan, and all my grown-up grandchildren—with love.

Special thanks to my daughter, Jessica North, for her practical help with the original idea; my goddaughter, Averil Dostine, for her enthusiasm and organisational and electronic skills; and Sharon Pie for her cooking expertise with children. Thank you, too, to the very special children who adventurously tested the recipes: Lucy and William Carpenter, Max Dostine, Martin and Lachlan Foote, Oliver and Hamish Harvey, Jessica Kerr, Rebecca Lee, and Nina Matsumoto. I also wish to thank my publisher, Catharine Retter, who has a heart for books and authors, as well as much patience!

First published by Citrus Press in Australia 2005
Recipes and additional text copyright © Carol Odell
Illustrations © Anna Pignataro

The Voyages of Dr. Dolittle © Hugh Lofting, published by permission
of Christopher Lofting c/- Ralph M. Vicinanza, Ltd.
Extract from *Winnie the Pooh* © A. A. Milne. Copyright under the Berne Convention.
Published by Egmont Books Limited, London and used with permission.

Sleeping Bear Press®
315 E. Eisenhower Parkway, Ste. 200
Ann Arbor, MI 48108
www.sleepingbearpress.com

© 2010 Sleeping Bear Press is an imprint of Gale, a part of Cengage Learning.

Printed and bound in the United States.

10 9 8 7 6 5 4 3 2

Library of Congress Cataloging-in-Publication Data

Odell, Carol.
Once upon a time in the kitchen : recipes and tales from classic
childrens stories / Carol Odell, Anna Pignataro.
p. cm.
ISBN 978-1-58536-518-0
1. Cookery—Juvenile literature. 2. Children's stories—Juvenile literature.
3. Food in literature—Juvenile literature. I. Pignataro, Anna, 1965- II. Title.
TX652.5.O3634 2010
808.8'0355—dc22
2010006857

Printed by Bang Printing, Brainerd, MN, 2nd Ptg., 12/2010